Dear Edith and De Wayne,
Thank you for helping to make this
testimony possible, by allowing me to
experience the love of Christ through
your lives.   Love, Jeff

TRANSFER
OF
TRUST

JEFF ROSENAU

Belleville, Ontario, Canada

TRANSFER OF TRUST
Copyright © 2008, Jeffery L. Rosenau

ISBN: 978-1-55452-304-7

For more information, please contact:

Jeff Rosenau
14046 East Stanford Circle, I-6,
Aurora, Colorado 80015
USA

www.accountabilityministries.org

Guardian Books is an imprint of *Essence Publishing,* a Christian Book Publisher dedicated to furthering the work of Christ through the written word. For more information, contact:

20 Hanna Court, Belleville, Ontario, Canada K8P 5J2
Phone: 1-800-238-6376 • Fax: (613) 962-3055
E-mail: info@essence-publishing.com
Web site: www.essence-publishing.com

Table of Contents

Acknowledgments

I praise God for bringing five very special people into my life at different intervals between 1980 and 1984 as I struggled with deep depression and severe anxiety. These people are my late Uncle Bruce and Aunt Wilma, my close friends Edith and DeWayne Leppke, and Chester Westfall. God brought them alongside me to be my friends, to listen, to walk through my illness with me, and to love me. Each met my needs in significant ways, but the two things they all helped me to experience were the unconditional love of God and what it means to be an other-minded servant of Jesus Christ. I will always be grateful to each of them for the Christ-like love they patiently and graciously extended to me.

Speaking of other-minded servants, I want to thank another beloved friend, Candy Hein, for encouraging me to write this book and for her superb work in editing this manuscript.

I also extend much gratitude to my dear friends Kent Scroggs and Wendy Shumaker for their kindness and diligence in taking the time to read, edit, and make great suggestions for improving this book. I really appreciate their eye for detail and Wendy's encouragement for me to dig deeper and to share more.

Foreword

There are different causes of anxiety and depression, but a primary one is the way we think. Jeff Rosenau's vulnerability in revealing the thinking processes that debilitated him helps us see how thinking wrongly, as he did, has disastrous results. It is a story of wrong thinking corrected by right thinking. It is a story of self-help supplanted by God's help. It is a story of deep despair and of wonderful victory.

I have only known Jeff as the humble, godly person he has become. The example of his life is one I want others to see. He has learned to trust God and to love with God's love. The end of the journey he shares in this book is one that I would wish for everyone. It is not one where he now knows all of the answers, but one where he knows God who has all of the answers.

Not everyone's journey or depression is the same. Jeff's story of learning to trust God rather than himself in the midst of suffering is a wonderful example of what can happen when we hold onto Jesus Christ—even when we are tempted to let go. It is an important message whether we are depressed or not.

—Dr. David Osborn, Director
Doctor of Ministry Program
Denver Seminary

Introduction

"Unless the Lord had given me help, I would soon have dwelt in the silence of death. When I said, 'My foot is slipping,' your love, O Lord, supported me. When anxiety was great within me, your consolation brought joy to my soul."

Psalm 94:17-19

Twenty-eight years ago, beginning in 1980, I experienced an emotional illness that led to deep depression and severe anxiety that lasted every day and every night for four years.

Without my knowledge, God had enrolled me into what I refer to as my post-graduate study at Nebuchadnezzar University (I'll explain what that means later) as God knew I was in need of humility and in need of Him. I didn't have to live in a field and eat grass like Nebuchadnezzar, but I did lose my freedom. I became a prisoner of my mind. And the more I fought to be free—the more freedom I lost.

I'd like to share how I experienced the love of Christ during that illness and how His love compelled me to *transfer my trust* from myself to Him.

In those four years, God would teach me seven life-changing lessons. At the end of that time, God restored my health and blessed me with a complete and full recovery from my illness as I came to know the truth, Jesus Christ, who set me free. For twenty-four years, I have not needed further medication or counseling. I praise God and give Him all the glory! For apart from the grace of God, such a miracle would not have been possible.

The purpose of this book is to glorify God by sharing what He did for me. I pray that God will use my testimony to offer the hope of Jesus Christ to people who are experiencing anxiety or depression.

—*Jeff Rosenau*

"Praise be to the God and Father of our Lord Jesus Christ, the Father of compassion and the God of all comfort, who comforts us in all our troubles, so that we can comfort those in any trouble with the comfort we ourselves have received from God."

2 Corinthians 1:3-4

Background for Chapter 1

A Train Is Coming

How serious was my illness? Why did I experience such fear and hopelessness? Why was I so introspective and unable to function during my illness? I hope the following analogy will provide some insight.

You're at home on a cool fall evening. You're blessed to have one of those much-needed alone times—just you and a good book—one you've been wanting to read for a long time.

The wood is cracklin' in the fireplace—you're in your favorite chair—feet propped up on the ottoman. You begin to read—no distractions. In your relaxed state, you are completely focused and immersed in this captivating story.

Now consider a different scene. You still have the same good book, the same captivating story you've been wanting to read. But instead of sitting in that comfortable chair in the safety of your home, imagine yourself tied to a railroad track. You don't hear a train coming or any noise at all for that matter. Are you able to concentrate on the words in the book? Why not? Try to relax and read the book. Are you distracted by the fear of a train coming? As hard as you may try to focus on the words, your mind and emotions cannot. You have only one interest—getting off the railroad track.

Suddenly, in the distance you hear a loud whistle as the train approaches, just a few miles away. Why can't you read like you normally do? What's wrong? You hear the train rumbling down the track, getting closer and closer. As you lean your head sideways, through the corner of one eye you catch a glimpse of the train. It's less than fifty yards away and traveling fast. Is there anything on your mind except fear and looking for a way of escape?

During my illness, the level of anxiety varied, but in my mind I was always on the track and knew the train was coming—no one could convince me otherwise. Anxiety from my perceived fear was as traumatic and painful as the real fear one would experience in the above scenario.

My train consisted of several railroad cars coming towards me, in the form of various fears. They included the fear of my dad's anger, the fear of being unorganized, the fear of public speaking, the fear of getting sick and dying, and the greatest fear of all—that I had committed the "unpardonable sin" (Matthew 12:22-32) and would be separated from God forever.

THE UNPARDONABLE SIN OR DIVINE CHASTENING?

In case you're wondering why I thought I had committed the "unpardonable sin," I'll try to explain. As a child, I had heard God's plan of salvation and always believed in Jesus Christ, but I never really knew Him, especially as Lord of my life.

Then after my dad died, Mom took us to different churches so I not only lost my source of truth from the Christ-centered, Bible-teaching church my dad took us to, but I also lost my primary source of discipline—my dad, as Mom was not a disciplinarian.

In an effort to be accepted by my peers, I did many sinful things that are common to rebellious teenagers. I then began to develop a pattern of confession and what seemed to be sincere repentance. However, as I look back, I consider my attempts at repentance more about me trying to avoid consequences of sin rather than having true repentance that includes godly sorrow, brokenness, and a sincere turning from sin.

After I got married and had children, the Holy Spirit was convicting me of my need to grow up and become a godly husband and father, as He knew I was still very immature in Christ. But many of my fears and insecurities, which I didn't share with anyone, began to resurface and kept me from responding in obedience to God.

This is hard to explain, but the following is what I believe took place, but won't know for sure until I get to heaven. God knew everything about me, including my fears and my manipulative ways, yet He loved me enough to help correct my way of thinking. He knew exactly what I needed, if I was ever to *become the person He is calling me to be.* Therefore, as part of God's divine chastening, I believe He turned me over to Satan, *so that my sinful nature may be destroyed, but my spirit saved* (1 Corinthians 5:5).

Immediately thereafter, Satan deceived me into believing I had committed the unpardonable sin, which I had inaccurately understood to mean that I had ignored the conviction of the Holy Spirit to the point that God's grace and forgiveness were no longer available to me. From that point on, a spirit or spirits of fear would torment my mind for the next four years.

There was a point in my illness when I felt like I was very close to losing touch with reality because the fear of being separated from God was so real and paralyzing. I felt out of control, helpless, and no longer of value or use to anyone. Those feelings led to deep depression, and there were times I no longer wanted to live. Knowing I needed help, I checked myself into a mental hospital.

After I checked in, a patient approached me and asked who my psychiatrist was. When I told her she said, "Oh he's the best. All of his patients get well." Somewhat comforted by her confidence, I settled in for my first night in the hospital. Remember my greatest fear and the main reason for my anxiety? I believed that I had committed the unpardonable sin, thinking I would be separated from God forever. As I lay in the darkened room with unfamiliar surroundings, all I would hear that night were the cries of a woman a few rooms down the hall, "I'm going to hell. I'm going to hell." Her screaming brought on more anguish for me that night, and any encouragement I had received from the patient's words about my doctor vanished quickly.

One might wonder why, if I didn't yet have a close relationship with God, the thought of being separated from Him would even bother me and why that possibility would cause me so much fear and anguish. I'm not certain, but I think the reason is that although I did not know God intimately, I believe I knew enough truth about God and His Son to know I needed Him. I just didn't know how great the need was. And that is one of the awesome miracles of God's grace. **Even when I was sinning and living life apart from God, *He pursued me*. God creates circumstances that draw us near to Him so He can transform our lives; giving us hope rather than despair—love instead of resentment and bitterness—joy in place of depression—and peace as opposed to fear or anxiety.**

Near the end of my four-year illness, God graciously helped me understand that the only sin that is unpardonable is the sin of failing to believe in and receive Jesus Christ as one's personal Savior and Lord before they die.

SHIFTING MY SOURCE OF HOPE

After a month in the hospital, I checked myself out. I tried to work, but the anxiety continued to get worse. If you recall my analogy of being tied to the railroad track, my preoccupation with trying to escape the fear I was experiencing was keeping me from functioning as a mature, responsible adult. I could no longer concentrate on the work I was doing and had to leave my job. With that inability to provide for my family came more hopelessness and despair. I had lost my sense of purpose and direction.

One night as I was driving, the fear became so intense I had a difficult time keeping my eyes on the road. Desperation drove me to the nearest exit. I pulled into the parking lot of what I believed was a mental hospital. I walked in and asked to be admitted. They kindly and calmly informed me that they couldn't as I was at a hospital for the mentally retarded. They informed me that there was a medical hospital not far away. Slightly embarrassed, I took their advice and proceeded on to that hospital. When I arrived, I asked them to give me something for the anxiety. I don't know what they gave me. I just know it was a strong dose, and I was out quickly.

But the reprieve was short-lived. The next morning I hallucinated, the one and only time in my life. I was being pulled into hell with all the fire and torment you can imagine. It was like a funnel, wide at the top and narrow at the bottom—dark black inside with fiery flames swirling all around—and I was being spun around and around and sucked downward into a bottomless pit of utter darkness. I yelled for help, but there was none. There were no people anywhere. Then I woke up.

I believe that God allowed the woman screaming down the hall and the hallucinations to clearly convey to me the reality of hell as a place of torment and total darkness and for me to gain an understanding of what it would be like to be hopelessly separated from God, for all eternity. To this day, those experiences serve as powerful reminders to me of what God's salvation saves us from, especially the irreversible eternal separation from God.

With the anxiety and depression only getting worse, I checked myself back into the mental hospital. My second stay only served to make me more uneasy as I watched patient after patient return—patients of my doctor. This was an eerie experience as I recalled the words from the other patient, "Oh he's the best. All his patients get well."

It didn't take long for me to realize that psychotherapy was not what I needed. I didn't believe I would ever get well again. But I knew with all my heart, as a result of hearing the gospel and the Word of God in Sunday school as a child, that if there was the slightest hope, it would come from me seeking and holding on to Jesus Christ.

I decided to leave the hospital and get the help I needed. But when I told my doctor I wanted to leave his response was, "You can't leave. You're not ready yet."

Unsatisfied with the doctor's response, I called the administrator of the hospital and said, "I checked myself into this hospital. Now I want to check myself out of here."

The next time I saw my doctor he said, "You can go now."

I checked out, called my aunt and uncle who had been missionaries for thirty-five years, and asked if they would be willing to help me. Of all the people I knew, I believed they had the closest relationship with the Lord. I respected their faith in Him. They didn't hesitate. I said an excruciatingly sad farewell to my wife and two young sons whom I loved deeply, got on a plane and flew from Michigan to South Carolina. I saw no other option, as I was too sick to help myself. And my wife had been so impacted by my illness that she was becoming emotionally drained herself and needed to stay healthy for our children's sake.

It was as though I was sentenced to prison and ripped away from my family. And in a sense I was—held captive to the anxiety and depression—until Jesus Christ would set me free. I lost my wife during the ordeal, as she gave up hope that I would ever be well again. She divorced me during the time I was gone. But God graciously reunited my sons and me a year later. Next to Jesus, they remain my closest friends and greatest blessing. I praise God for the great honor of being a father to such wonderful sons as Rob and Travis.

In 1984, four long years after the anxiety and depression had begun, God instantly and miraculously healed me. For the last eighteen years, I have served as president of Accountability Ministries. God has blessed me with the honor of serving as one of His messengers—teaching Biblical principles that challenge, encourage, and prepare God's children to *become the people God is calling us to be.*

How Did I Get Well?

There are many labels given to people suffering with emotional illness, such as "manic-depressive" and "obsessive-compulsive," to name a couple. But God would help me to understand that the best description of my illness was "emotional and spiritual immaturity."

God used my four-year illness to come alongside and help me to mature. He knew I wouldn't be able to complete this journey alone, so at different intervals of the illness, God mercifully and sovereignly brought some very special people alongside me: my late Uncle Bruce and Aunt Wilma, dear friends Edith and DeWayne Leppke and Chester Westfall.

God would use each of their lives to help me experience His unconditional love.

On this journey, the seven life-changing lessons that God taught me are:

- God's love includes discipline and accountability.

- God's love reveals truth is a person.

- God's love makes faith possible.

- God's love is intimate.

- God's love extends grace and forgiveness.

- God's love exhorts us to surrender and transfer our trust to Him.

- God's love compels us to follow His Son.

Ultimately, God would use my illness to convey His love for me in deep, intimate ways, enabling me to *transfer my trust* from myself to Him.

REVIEW

1. Going from left to right, circle the word(s) that best describe what you are experiencing most, at this point in your life.

HOPE	or	DESPAIR
LOVE	or	RESENTMENT & BITTERNESS
JOY	or	DEPRESSION
PEACE	or	FEAR & ANXIETY

2. List any fears that you have.

    _____

    _____

    _____

3. Are any of those fears causing you anxiety. If so, which ones?

    _____

    _____

    _____

4. If you are struggling with anxiety or depression, who are the people in your life who you can go to for prayer, encouragement, and unconditional love?

    _____

    _____

    _____

Chapter 1

Who's in Control of My Mind?

"Those who live according to the sinful nature have their minds set on what that nature desires; but those who live in accordance with the Spirit have their minds set on what the Spirit desires. The mind of sinful man is death, but the mind controlled by the Spirit is life and peace; the sinful mind is hostile to God. It does not submit to God's law, nor can it do so. Those controlled by the sinful nature cannot please God."

Romans 8:5-8

I remember during my childhood years that every time my dad went to work on any kind of project around the house, fear would grip my mother, brother, and me.

Dad would always be missing at least one tool necessary to complete the project, and many times I was falsely accused of misplacing that tool. My dad had a pretty loud voice and scared me when he was angry. I didn't like the fear or the injustice, so I tried to put a plan of action together to relieve our family of these conflicts. I decided to hide my dad's tools. From that point on, whenever dad needed a tool I retrieved it for him, as I always knew exactly where it was.

I never told my dad what I had done.

One evening when I was nine years old, my dad was getting ready for work. He went into the bathroom and threw up blood. As he walked out of the bathroom, he grabbed his briefcase. My mom saw the blood and confronted Dad: "Where do you think you're going?"

He replied, "To work, someone has to make the money."

My dad then walked across the kitchen floor, sat down at the table and his eyes rolled back until all you could see were the whites of his eyes. Mom said, "Stop kidding around, Lowell." But it was no joke. Something was wrong—very wrong—and Mom quickly called an ambulance.

I never saw my dad again. Two days later, he died from a bleeding ulcer.

Thoughts and emotions raced through my mind—relief and sadness. Relief, as I was afraid of my father's temper, yet great sadness as the man whose love and attention I desired the most was gone.

How could I prevent what caused my father's death from happening to me?

I thought about the last words I heard my father speak, "To work, someone has to make the money." Questions and more irrational fears flooded my mind. What caused my father's anger? Will anger kill you? What did work and money have to do with anything? Then I remembered how my dad would get angry if he couldn't find a tool, as I explained earlier. This persuaded me even more that if my father wasn't in control of circumstances, he would become angry.

So my logic as a nine-year-old went like this: *"I must now be in control and avoid becoming angry because if I lose control and become angry, death will surely follow."* This thinking caused me to deny or repress anger and to fear being unorganized and out of control.

These experiences contributed to me becoming a well-organized perfectionist, to having an irrational fear of being disorganized, and to becoming a hypochondriac. But I couldn't seem to ever get organized enough to alleviate the anxiety. Therefore, I would try harder.

Once again, I didn't share this reasoning with anyone, as to do so would have meant trusting someone other than myself. I perceived such vulnerability to be too risky—*a relinquishing of control.*

This began the path of trusting in myself and my immature logic, rather than trusting anyone else, including God. It was a means of control—of attempting to circumvent fear, pain, anger, injustice. For the next twenty-some years, *I trusted no one except myself* to watch out for me. As you can imagine, I made a lot of mistakes.

Over time, God helped me realize I was born with the need for love, acceptance, and affirmation. When those needs were not met, I hurt. I became preoccupied with removing the pain. I began to search for ways to relieve the pain. It is then that I had to decide who or what to trust in and depend upon to relieve my misery. I had only two choices:

1. **Trust myself and be controlled by the sinful nature.**
   (By turning to drugs, sex outside of marriage, alcohol abuse, lying, "people pleasing," or other sinful behavior to relieve the pain.)

2. **Trust Jesus Christ and be controlled by the Holy Spirit.**
   (By turning to God and obeying Him so that fear

and anxiety are replaced with peace—and depression with joy.)

NEBUCHADNEZZAR UNIVERSITY

With God's help, I would eventually learn that I was being *controlled by my sinful nature* when placing my trust in myself rather than trusting God. That's called pride.

What does God's Word say about pride? In Proverbs, we gain some insight:

> "Pride goes before destruction, a haughty spirit before a fall" (Proverbs 16:18).

> "A man's pride will bring him low, but a humble spirit will obtain honor" (Proverbs 29:23, NASB).

The pride of thinking I could live life apart from God was keeping me spiritually immature. My immature response to my fears would eventually be replaced with the mature response of faith in God as I came to know, trust, and obey Him.

But if we continue in our pride, God will take the initiative to bring this to our attention. In the book of Daniel, we find a story about Nebuchadnezzar, the king of the entire Babylonian empire. He was a very proud man. One day he had a dream and asked Daniel to interpret it, which Daniel did with these words:

> "This is the interpretation, O king, and this is the decree of the Most High, which has come upon my lord the king: that you be driven away from mankind, and your dwelling place be with the beasts of the field, and you be given grass to eat like cattle and be drenched with the dew of heaven; and seven periods of time will pass over you, until you recog-

nize that the Most High is ruler over the realm of mankind, and bestows it on whomever He wishes.

'Therefore, O king, may my advice be pleasing to you: break away now from your sins by doing righteousness, and from your iniquities by showing mercy to the poor, in case there may be a prolonging of your prosperity'" (Daniel 4:24-25, 27, NASB).

As I began to reflect on my experiences, I came to realize that the following wise counsel given to the king also applied to me, *"Break away now from your sins by doing righteousness...."*

As God did with Nebuchadnezzar, He had given me many gracious opportunities to repent of living a life apart from Him and His will for me. If I had been wise, I would have humbly paid attention to the gentle conviction of sin that I received from the Holy Spirit on prior occasions, repented, and learned the easier way. But I had more fear of man than of God. The people I had to live with each day were real, and God was still unknown to me as a relational heavenly Father. Because I didn't know God or His nature as He truly is, I didn't trust Him. Because I didn't know and trust Him, I rarely had enough wisdom and courage to obey Him. Therefore, it was necessary for me to learn the hard way as did Nebuchadnezzar, according to Daniel 4:28-30, NASB:

"All this happened to Nebuchadnezzar the king. Twelve months later he was walking on the roof of the royal palace of Babylon. The king reflected and said, 'Is this not Babylon the great, which I myself have built as a royal residence by the might of my power and for the glory of my majesty?'"

Pride at its peak. *"Which I myself have built"*—*"by the might of my power and for the glory of my majesty."* I, my, and my. Selfish, self-centered pride. No glory given to God, just himself.

God, through Daniel had informed Nebuchadnezzar what would happen unless he recognized that the Most High is ruler over the realm of mankind and bestows it on whomever he wishes.

But Nebuchadnezzar ignored God—and failed to repent. To learn the consequences, let's pick up the story beginning with Daniel 4:31:

> "While the word was in the king's mouth, a voice came from heaven, saying, 'King Nebuchadnezzar, to you it is declared: sovereignty has been removed from you, and you will be driven away from mankind, and your dwelling place will be with the beasts of the field. You will be given grass to eat like cattle, and seven periods of time will pass over you, until you recognize that the Most High is ruler over the realm of mankind, and bestows it on whomever He wishes.'
>
> Immediately the word concerning Nebuchadnezzar was fulfilled; and he was driven away from mankind and began eating grass like cattle, and his body was drenched with the dew of heaven, until his hair had grown like eagles' feathers and his nails like birds' claws" (Daniel 4:31-33, NASB).

Due to Nebuchadnezzar's pride in saying that the success he had experienced was achieved by his power and for his own glory, God removed his ability to reason and Nebuchadnezzar's life went out of control. He became powerless.

I could really relate to Nebuchadnezzar as my life went out of control and I too lost my ability to function as a normal human being. Although in different ways, I was no less a captive than Nebuchadnezzar—powerless to set myself free—powerless to regain my reason until God chose to give it back to me. To be left so helpless was not only frightening but extremely depressing.

Numerous times during my four-year illness, I wanted to die. I saw myself as worthless—of no value to anyone. In the mental hospital, I took the prescribed medication for depression just to make me sleep, so I would not have to face living in such a pitiful condition.

Separated from my wife and sons while in South Carolina, I wondered if I would ever see them again. Though we talked on the phone each week, wrote letters, and I did provide for them with disability income, it was awful being apart from each other.

For Easter, I sent my sons two soccer balls. I later got a picture of my wife with our sons smiling while holding onto those soccer balls. Behind their smiles, I could see in their faces the look of my sons saying, "Where are you, Dad? We miss you. We love you. We need you." And as I studied my wife, dressed in a lovely pink dress and smiling, I saw the face of the woman I married—the face of a person who was tired and worn out— the face of a person who was going through the most traumatic experience of her life. I was to blame for their suffering, the suffering of people I loved more than anyone else. To this day, I cannot look at that photo without getting tears in my eyes.

I so desperately wanted to "snap out of it" and be there for my family. Because I had no power to do so, I didn't want to live. I didn't even want to get out of bed. Only my uncle's daily persistence forced me out of bed. He made me walk around the block, day after day. He gave me books on emotional healing. My aunt and uncle took me to church with them, made time to listen to me, pray for me, love me. Still, my inability to set myself free, to regain my reason, and to overcome my hopelessness continued.

During the third year of my illness, and having been separated from my family for several months, I received a letter saying that my wife had filed for divorce, which was even more devastating. Though unexpected, I didn't blame her. She too was young in her faith and was not getting the godly counsel she needed. She likely had given up hope that I would ever recover and wanted to protect her own emotional well-being for the sake of our children. I understood, as I also believed I would never be well again.

Due to my low self-esteem, immaturity, and inability to overcome my depression, I didn't know how to respond. Though I knew marriage was to be for as long as we both shall live, I felt they deserved better. As much as I longed to be the person my family deserved, that person didn't exist at that time. I was far from being the husband, the dad, *the person God was calling me to be.*

MY REASON RETURNED TO ME

"But at the end of that period I, Nebuchadnezzar, raised my eyes toward heaven, and my reason returned to me, and I blessed the Most High and praised and honored Him who lives forever;

For His dominion is an everlasting dominion,

And His kingdom endures from generation to generation.

And all the inhabitants of the earth are accounted as nothing,

But He does according to His will in the host of heaven

And among the inhabitants of earth;

And no one can ward off His hand

Or say to Him, 'What hast thou done?'

At that time my reason returned to me. And my majesty and splendor were restored to me for the glory of my kingdom, and my counselors and my nobles began seeking me out; so I was reestablished in my sovereignty, and surpassing greatness was added to me.

Now I Nebuchadnezzar praise, exalt, and honor the King of heaven, for all His works are true and His ways just, and He is able to humble those who walk in pride" (Daniel 4:34-37, NASB).

In Daniel 4, verses 34 and 36 Nebuchadnezzar makes a statement worth noting, *"My reason returned to me."*

When did his reason return? After he humbled himself and *raised his eyes toward heaven* (v. 34), recognizing his need for God, and when he *blessed the Most High and praised and honored Him*, acknowledging God's sovereignty.

"Draw near to God and He will draw near to you" (James 4:8a, NASB).

Lesson #1

God's Love Includes Discipline and Accountability

My dad was a disciplinarian, and I longed for the loving correction he would have administered, had he not died. For years after losing my dad, I sought discipline from people in authority. Though I begged for discipline for over twenty years, the chastisement never came until 1980. It was then that my heavenly Father intervened to show me that He loved me enough to take me aside and personally administer the discipline and accountability I needed so desperately.

As He did with Nebuchadnezzar, God used discipline to humble me—to help me know Him intimately—and to prepare me to *transfer my trust* from myself to Him.

I remember as a young person doing something wrong and then praying very sincerely to God, "If you get me out of this, I will never do it again, I promise."

God seemed to graciously protect me from the errors of my way, but my faithfulness would only last a few months, and I'd find myself praying the same prayer, "If you get me out of this, I'll never do it again. I'm serious this time."

I think I truly meant what I said, but there was a spiritual problem that was a barrier to my obedience. The problem was that I knew about Jesus, but I didn't know Him personally. And if I didn't know Jesus, how could I trust Him—or obey Him?

This begging and pleading and breaking my promises to God continued for many years.

In order to correct that behavior, God helped me to recognize my inability to manipulate or control anything. He would make it clear to me that life is not a game, but a serious journey here on earth. He would help me come to know Him; not only as the merciful and compassionate Father that He is, but also as a God of justice, who hates sin.

I was later to learn that God used my emotional illness to show me His love and plan for my life. Looking back, I now understand that the suffering I experienced was allowed by a holy and righteous Father to help me hit bottom, look up, and see my desperate need for Him.

God's loving discipline kept me so close and dependent upon Him that I learned to trust Him. Any other route would have destroyed my life. I knew with certainty that Jesus alone was my only hope. I recall the pain of the emotional illness was almost unbearable, yet necessary. It drew me into an intimate relationship with the true and living God.

"My son, do not reject the discipline of the Lord,
Or loathe His reproof,
For whom the Lord loves He reproves,
Even as a father, the son in whom he delights."
Proverbs 3:11-12, NASB

"FOR THOSE WHOM THE LORD LOVES HE DISCIPLINES…"
Hebrews 12:6, NASB

TRANSFER OF TRUST

Father, thank You for helping me understand that my mind was being controlled by my sinful nature, but that I had another option. I could submit to You, set my mind on and be controlled by what the Holy Spirit desires—and experience life and peace, if only I would humble myself and trust You.

Thank you for teaching me that Your discipline was evidence of Your love for me. Thank You for using that discipline to keep me close and dependent upon You. I praise You for allowing the pain that comes with anxiety and depression to draw me into an intimate relationship with You so that I could come to know and trust You. In Jesus' name, amen.

NEXT

In chapter two, I share ways in which God would continue taking me from darkness to light—from being deceived and trusting in myself to a knowledge of the truth and the trustworthy source of all truth.

REVIEW

1. Read Romans 8:5-8. What can you learn from that passage of Scripture about how to experience life and peace?

    _____

    _____

    _____

2. Read the section under subtitle, *Misplaced Trust/Imaginary Control.* Identify and explain how any of your traumatic childhood experiences may have contributed to you trusting in yourself and wanting to be in control.

    _____

    _____

    _____

3. Emotional needs of people include love, acceptance, and affirmation. It hurts when those needs are not met. When those needs are not being met in your life, who or what do you *turn to and trust in* to relieve the pain?

    _____

    _____

    _____

4. Do you know God well enough to *trust and obey* Him? If no, why do you think that is?

    _____

    _____

    _____

If yes, what *attributes* of God cause you to love, trust and obey Him?

_____

_____

_____

5. If you are experiencing anxiety or depression and are unable to "snap out of it", read the sections under subtitles *Nebuchadnezzar University* and *My Reason Returned to Me*.

    What can you learn from those sections about recovering from an emotional illness?

    _____

    _____

    _____

6. Would you describe the discipline you received while growing up as too harsh, too lenient, or loving? If it was harsh or too lenient, how might that hinder your ability to understand that discipline from God is *evidence of His love for you?*

    _____

    _____

    _____

Chapter 2

Do I Know the Truth?

"Behold, Thou dost desire truth in the innermost being,
And in the hidden part Thou wilt make me know wisdom."

Psalm 51:6, NASB

FROM IGNORANCE TO A KNOWLEDGE OF THE TRUTH

This journey that I'm sharing was never so much about me pursuing God as it was about *God pursuing me*. His desire was for me to come to a knowledge of the truth—to a knowledge of Himself.

Why did God desire truth in my innermost being? Because He knew all the ways in which I had been deceived and how believing lies was affecting my life in negative ways. See some examples on the next page.

Lies I Believed	Results of Believing Those Lies
That my dad's anger and him being unorganized caused his death. So if I didn't repress my anger and become well organized and in control, I'd likely die, too.	I became a well-organized perfectionist, with fear of being unorganized and out of control. I became a hypochondriac with fear of death. Life was not enjoyable.
That I committed the "unpardonable sin" and was separated from God forever.	Severe anxiety and deep depression that paralyzed me and destroyed my marriage.
That I was incapable of speaking well in front of an audience because I likely wouldn't know what to say or how to say it, look stupid, and embarrass myself.	Fear of public speaking that prevented me from having opportunities to communicate with groups of people and share what might benefit others.

God knew that if there was any hope of this cycle being broken and any hope of me being set free of these various bondages, it would happen as a result of me coming to know the truth and appropriating that truth in my life. God also knew that in order for me to live my life based on truth, the *transfer of trust* from myself to Him was critical.

But before that *transfer of trust* could take place, it was

~~Lent Revival~~
Miss Margaret Euren
~~Creative~~

II Peter 1
vs 3-10

1 Peter 1

vs 3-10

imperative that I first come to know His Son. The reason, as I would learn later, is that *Jesus is the truth* who sets people free.

During my illness, I never understood all this so clearly. But now I see that it wasn't so much that I was pursuing truth as it was *God pursuing me* to bring me to a knowledge of His truth, to a knowledge of Himself through His Son so I would learn to trust Him and obey Him.

> "For it is God who works in you to will and to act according to his good purpose" (Philippians 2:13).

I would come to understand that it was not enough to know the words of God. I would need to know and trust the God who inspired all Scripture to be written (2 Timothy 3:16, NKJV). For if I didn't know and trust Him, why would I believe His Word to be true?

Before I came to know and understand how much Jesus loves me, it didn't matter how many times I read and re-read Philippians 4:6-7 about the peace of God replacing anxious thoughts, my anxiety didn't go away.

Until I came to know my heavenly Father truly does love and accept me as a forgiven child of His, it made little difference in my life that the Bible says "Believe in the Lord Jesus, and you will be saved" (Acts 16:31).

For many years I had been deceived and didn't know it. As I searched for answers, I learned of two essential prerequisites to discovering the truth—repentance and accepting the certainty of my salvation through faith.

As I began to understand how my sins of fear, anger, pride, and my lack of faith in God grieved the Holy Spirit, I became truly sorry for my sins and repented. I then became able to discern spiritual truths as I read and meditated on God's Word. No longer was the Bible simply another book with ink on paper. I began to understand with my heart what I already knew in my head, that the Bible actually is *the living Word of God* (Hebrews 4:12). With fellowship restored, I could now hear my heavenly Father speaking to me. I began to know Him—to understand His heart, His interests, His love for sinners like me—and His will for my life.

I began to pray as David did when he was suffering with anxiety and depression, "Search me, O God, and know my heart; test me and know my anxious thoughts. See if there is any offensive way in me, and lead me in the way everlasting" (Psalm 139:23-24).

As God searched me, hidden sins were brought into the light. The brighter the light, the more I could see like Jeremiah that *the heart is deceitful above all things* (Jeremiah 17:9). Until then, I had never comprehended how truly sinful I was—and how much I had hurt God, my heavenly Father who had been waiting so patiently—day after day, year after year—for me to return to Him.

As the Holy Spirit worked within my heart to move me *from ignorance to a knowledge of the truth*, I began to realize how deceived I had been for so many years.

Like my dad, I didn't trust and obey the wisdom available to me from my heavenly Father. Instead, I believed and acted on what I thought would best protect me. This was prideful and self-centered thinking.

My sinful nature and the influence of this world led me to believe I should hide my weaknesses and reveal my strengths. This type of thinking kept me from acknowledging my negative emotions. Being deceived in that way blinded me to my need for repentance.

To help me understand how deceived I had been about weakness, the Holy Spirit gently helped me comprehend how significantly different God's ways are than our ways.

One such example came as I listened to Jesus' unique words in regard to weakness, "My grace is sufficient for you, for my power is made perfect in weakness."

To which Paul replied, "Therefore I will boast all the more gladly about my weaknesses, so that Christ's power may rest on me" (2 Corinthians 12:9).

SHARING WEAKNESS

Was God telling me that weaknesses could be good? Indeed He was. Let me share an example from my youth to illustrate this principle.

When I was a sophomore in high school, we had a class meeting to elect new class officers for the following year. Totally to my surprise my best friend nominated me for class president. That was bad enough, but what made it worse was I won the election.

Winning meant I would have to speak in front of the whole class the following year. Like many people, I had a fear of public speaking. Do you remember having to give those oral book reports in school? I do, and I always volunteered to go first. That way, I didn't have to sit there nervously waiting my turn as others spoke.

The next year rolled around, and it was time for our first meeting, with me as president, in front of the entire class. For days, I kept going over my notes—frequently bugging my class advisor with questions as to what I was supposed to say and do.

Finally, the big day arrived. Anxiously reviewing my notes, I walked over to my class advisor to ask just one last question. He was a big man, our wrestling coach, and a teacher whom I respected. Before I got the question out of my mouth, he interrupted me with words of reassurance, "Just go do it." It sounded as though he had confidence in me. Sensing his support and affirmation, I took his advice. I went and did it—and truly enjoyed the moment.

Inside, I was still that little nine-year-old boy in need of a "father" figure to tell me, "You can do it"—to believe in me—to have the security of knowing I would still be loved and accepted even when I took these first steps toward public speaking.

But the sad part of this story came later.

Class presidents could not serve consecutive terms. I thought of the possibility of someone nominating me again for president our senior year. If elected, that would include public speaking at our graduation ceremony, not just to my class which I enjoyed, but to the entire student body, including parents. With my warped thinking and fear of public speaking, I told myself, *"To eliminate the risk of anyone considering me for president our senior year, I'm not going to be so friendly to people any more. That should solve the problem."*

The strategy worked, but at great cost. I had successfully avoided facing my fear, but didn't realize what a foothold I'd given Satan. From that point on and for many years thereafter, I avoided anything to do with public speaking because of fear. It became a huge barrier to me *becoming the person God intended me to be.*

For years, my fear of failure had led me to wrongly place trust in myself to come up with ways to avoid rejection. That foothold of Satan's fueled another sin—the sin of pride. I wouldn't share my weaknesses. I'd only let people see what appeared to be strengths. But the truth was that many of the things I perceived to be signs of strength were not. Sharing my weaknesses with others would have taken much more courage than trying to conceal them.

Only years later, as I learned to replace my fear with faith in God and to share my weaknesses, would those strongholds Satan had in my life eventually be destroyed.

Ironically, God's will and purpose for my life was to be one of His messengers—not because of any strength or skill of my own in public speaking, but because He loves and accepts me as I am and His grace is sufficient for me. Again—humility and availability to God versus pride.

I didn't need to be a strong dynamic speaker or believe in my ability to speak, I needed to believe in the One who I trusted to love, accept, and affirm me whether I spoke well, or poorly, then humbly submit to His will and purposes for my life. The fact that He now uses me in this area of weakness is another miraculous testimony to His grace.

Lesson #2

God's Love Reveals Truth is a Person

As I searched for truth—I would eventually discover that it was actually a search for Jesus Christ, and a desire to know Him.

One day while visiting my aunt and uncle, I noticed a picture frame. Enclosed under the glass were these two passages of Scripture:

"Jesus answered, 'I am the way and the truth and the life....'"
John 14:6

"Then you will know the truth, and
the truth will set you free."
John 8:32

It began to register even more clearly: **Jesus Himself is the truth who will set me free—keep holding on to Him.**

Transfer of Trust

Father, thank You for revealing truth in my innermost being and for making me know Your wisdom in the hidden part of my mind. I praise You for loving me enough to reveal that Jesus is the truth who would set me free from a life of being deceived so that I could start walking in the truth. In Jesus' name, amen.

Next

In chapter three I'm faced with a choice, fear or faith?

My anxiety was paralyzing and keeping me from enjoying life and from *becoming the person God is calling me to be*. But God's love made faith possible. His love enabled me to place my faith in Him, and my fears began to vanish.

REVIEW

1. On page 36, look at the chart with the headings, *Lies I Believed* and *Results of Believing Those Lies.* Have you been deceived into believing any of those three lies? If so, what have been the results of believing those lies?

_____

_____

_____

2. In the chart below, list other lies you have believed and the results of believing those lies.

Lies I Believed	Results of Believing Those Lies

3. Read the section under the subtitle, *Sharing Weakness.* What weaknesses do you have that you have not been willing to share with anyone?

_____

_____

_____

4. Who or what is your primary *source of truth* that you place your trust in, and why do you believe that source is reliable?

_____

_____

_____

5. Read John 14:6, then John 8:32. How well do you know Jesus Christ? Who is He to you, and why is it important for you to know Him if you want to be free of anxiety and depression?

_____

_____

_____

Chapter 3

Fear or Faith?

"Be anxious for nothing, but in everything by prayer and supplication with thanksgiving let your requests be made known to God. And the peace of God, which surpasses all comprehension, shall guard your hearts and your minds in Christ Jesus."

Philippians 4:6-7, NASB

As a child I was almost never sick, but those around me were. My brother was taken to the hospital to have his appendix out and was gone for several days. Later he had to have an operation on his leg, and he said it really hurt him. My dad had arthritis in his back and took heavy medication daily for the pain. He developed a bleeding ulcer, went to the hospital, and died at age thirty-four. On two occasions after Dad passed away, I recall coming home from school to find a note lying on the kitchen counter from my mother. Each note simply explained that she had gone to the hospital and for me to call the person listed on the paper. That scared me. A hospital took my brother away from me for several days. A hospital took my dad away for good, and who knew if a hospital would take my mom away—and for how long?

Keep in mind that all these events took place between the ages of five and nine, and the misunderstanding came from the *immature* logic of my young mind.

I told myself I wanted nothing to do with being sick or getting ill in any way and that hospitals were places that hurt you—not healed you. They separated you from your loved ones—sometimes permanently. As a result, I developed a fear of injury, illness, or disease that might send me to that dreaded institution called a hospital.

Emotional and Spiritual Immaturity

While working as an insurance underwriter, I began to experience more symptoms of stress than usual. After hearing from various media that stress could cause heart attacks and strokes, negative thoughts from my childhood would flood my mind. As the stress increased, the thoughts increased, which in turn increased the stress. The combination of stress and fear snowballed, causing my heart to race— rapid breathing—then loss of breath. I didn't have any idea what was happening to me.

The more those symptoms occurred, the more confused I became. I expected to have a heart attack or stroke and die. Instead, I was experiencing unexpected anxiety and hyperventilation.

I did everything I knew to control my own destiny and stop what was happening to me, but absolutely nothing worked. I only got worse.

The fast pace and stress became so bad that if I was driving and came to a green traffic light, I was okay. But if I drove up to a red light, I'd begin to hyperventilate. If I went to the grocery store and just one person was in the checkout line ahead of me, causing me to wait, I'd begin to hyperventilate.

I was too busy. Things needed to get done—lights and people were slowing me down. Each additional "little thing" was hindering me from being organized and in control of my circumstances. The challenges of daily living became too much for me to handle. I knew I was in trouble, but I didn't have the foggiest idea why or what to do about it.

So what would it take to break this cycle? Would I continue to hide my fears and avoid facing them? No, it was time to face them by gradually *transferring trust* in myself to trust in God.

> "When I was a child, I talked like a child, I thought like a child, I reasoned like a child. When I became a man, I put childish ways behind me" (1 Corinthians 13:11).

> "…we take captive every thought to make it obedient to Christ" (2 Corinthians 10:5).

RELINQUISHING CONTROL

A few years after recovering from my illness, God would give me opportunity to practice *transferring my trust* from myself to Him. The owner of a company I worked for had set up businesses in six different states. We were foolishly working eighty-plus hours each week, flying from one state to another and back again.

One day at the end of a long week, I boarded the airplane to go home. As I sat down and leaned back in my seat, it was such a shock to relax that I began to hyperventilate for the first time in many years.

Having come to know the trustworthiness of God, I immediately bowed my head and prayed, *"Father, I don't care if I die if that's your will. My life is yours and you're in control."*

God heard my prayer and graciously intervened. I stopped hyperventilating instantly and have never had an episode since.

All those years of hypochondria and suffering with fear of the unknown were due to me trying to control something which I had no control over. When I *transferred my trust* (control) to the One who is in control, the Lord Jesus Christ, my hypochondria and fear subsided, as God's peace filled my heart.

> "For God has not given us a spirit of fear, but of power and of love and of a sound mind" (2 Timothy 1:7, NKJV).

Lesson #3

God's Love Makes Faith Possible

Having known the way of salvation since a young child and even believing I had received Christ as a child, I still struggled with the assurance of my salvation. I thought God became so irritated with my game of manipulation that He finally gave up on me.

There wasn't any verse or counsel that would help. In my mind, I was convinced I had exhausted God's patience with me.

But one day, as I shared those feelings with my Uncle Bruce, he asked, "What does Romans 10:13 say?"

I replied, *"Everyone who calls on the name of the Lord will be saved."*

"Have you done that?," he asked.

"Yes," I answered.

To which my uncle boldly replied, **"Then God is stuck with you. It no longer matters what you think. God's word is that good."**

As I reflected on my uncle's wisdom—**"God's word is that good"**—it hit me. I didn't know God like my uncle did. I knew about God, but I didn't really know Him—especially as a **trustworthy Father—whose word is good.**

Having lost my earthly father at a young age, I hadn't experienced the trustworthiness of a father. But now I began to understand that my heavenly Father could be trusted. This was another important lesson God used to help me know Him better, and a critical breakthrough step in the process of God enabling me to *transfer trust* in myself to placing my trust in Him.

"Now this is eternal life: that they may know you, the only true God, and Jesus Christ, whom you have sent."

John 17:3

"You will keep him in perfect peace, whose mind is stayed on You, because he trusts in You."

Isaiah 26:3, NKJV

Transfer of Trust

Father, thank You for helping me come to know You as the trustworthy Father You are—whose word is good. Thank You for confirming that I am one of Your children—that You have graciously forgiven me of my sins—and have promised that I will spend eternity with You.

Because of Your faithfulness, my fears and anxiety have been replaced with the perfect peace of Christ. Thank You for giving me faith to trust You. In Jesus' name, amen.

NEXT

The truths in chapter four reveal God's nature even more clearly, helping me come to know Him as the merciful, compassionate, and loving Father that He is.

REVIEW

1. Read the section under subtitle, *Emotional and Spiritual Immaturity*. In what ways, if any, do you relate to what the author experienced?

   _____

   _____

   _____

2. Read the section under subtitle, *Relinquishing Control*. What challenge might God be presenting to you as an opportunity to relinquish control, and *transfer trust* in yourself to trust in Him? Explain why you think so, and how you believe God wants you to respond.

   _____

   _____

   _____

3. In reading *Transfer of Trust*, what have you learned about God that is different from how you had perceived Him to be?

   _____

   _____

   _____

4. Why is knowing the true nature and character of God integral to the process of *transferring trust* in yourself to placing your trust in Him?

   _____

   _____

   _____

Chapter 4

Does God Love Me?

"...God demonstrates his own love for us in this:
While we were still sinners, Christ died for us."

Romans 5:8

My dad was one of six sons born in the 1920s to missionary parents who served in Africa.

When missionary kids reached school age, their parents brought them back to the United States and left them in another family's care, so the children could attend school. In 1932, my dad and two of my uncles remained in America, while their parents returned to Africa. Uncle Gene was nine years old, my dad (Lowell) was eight, and Uncle Bruce seven.

A godly couple in the town I grew up in had agreed to care for all three boys. But shortly before my grandparents were to return to Africa, this couple changed their minds and explained that they would only be able to provide for two of the children. Well, time was running short, so Dad's parents had to quickly find another couple for one of the children. They did—and my dad ended up separated from his brothers.

My mom told me that this so-called Christian couple had treated my dad like a slave, working him from sun up to sun down. Imagine being eight years old—your parents have said goodbye and you know you won't see them again for four years—you're separated from your brothers—left all alone with strangers. On top of that, you're mistreated by the couple who were to love, nurture, and care for you.

Dad was later to find more love and acceptance from classmates in school who were not Christians. As he built relationships with those friends, he began to live as they did in ways that were not pleasing to God. Mom and Dad met in school and married in their late teens. Dad shipped out to serve in World War II the day after their wedding.

I have few memories of my dad—most are not good. I know he had rheumatoid arthritis in his back and was in much pain most of the time. He took cortisone and about thirty aspirin every day for the pain. He worked long hours and was seldom home. When he was home, his temper is what I remember most.

In the nine years I lived with my dad, I have few memories of him ever spending time with me or talking with me. Mostly he would yell at me for something I did wrong or that he assumed I did wrong.

Almost every Friday and Saturday night, he and Mom would party with their friends. My brother Fred and I were left to play with their friends' kids, while they drank and played cards.

Later in the evening, my brother and I were placed in some dark unfamiliar bedroom to sleep, usually on top of the covers along with the coats that had also been discarded there. Into the night, I'd listen to loud talking and joking as my parents enjoyed themselves with others. I felt insignificant and unloved. I so much wanted my mom and dad to spend time with me and to love me like they appeared to love their friends.

I have, however, held on to three fond memories, moments my dad took time to be a father. The first memory, when I was six years old, followed a spanking from my dad. Afterwards, he sat me on his lap, then calmly and gently explained why I needed that discipline. At that moment, *I felt loved.*

Another fond memory occurred when I was seven years old. One evening, Dad took me to a restaurant. Mom was recuperating from surgery in the hospital, and so it was just Dad and me—no one else. I remember having a bowl of chili with him. It's the only time in my life I recall being alone with my dad and having a peaceful one-to-one conversation. That night, *I felt significant and listened to.*

The third fond memory of my dad was when I was eight. I was walking home from school with an older boy when a disagreement took place and the kid tripped me. I fell on the pavement and cut my hand. When I returned home, Dad saw my bleeding hand and wanted to know what happened. After I explained, he immediately led me out to our car and we drove to the house of the boy and his parents. Dad took me to the door, knocked, and asked to see the boy and his dad. My father proceeded to let the parent know that such behavior better not happen again. I remember that evening in great detail. *I felt very secure.* My dad had defended me.

I felt loved by my father's discipline. I felt significant when my father listened to me and showed interest in what I had to say. I felt secure when my father defended me. Later on, I would discover that my heavenly Father also *disciplines, listens to, and defends* His children, as following verses confirm.

"Our fathers disciplined us for a little while as they thought best; but God disciplines us for our good, that we may share in his holiness" (Hebrews 12:10).

"If I had cherished sin in my heart, the Lord would not have listened; but God has surely listened and heard my voice in prayer" (Psalm 66:18-19).

"My dear children, I write this to you so that you will not sin. But if anybody does sin, we have one who speaks to the Father in our defense—Jesus Christ, the Righteous One" (1 John 2:1).

As my father's behavior influenced me, I assume that his parents and his foster caregivers influenced him. Remember my uncles, Bruce and Eugene, who stayed together with a godly couple who loved and nurtured them? They and their wives went on to serve as missionaries in Africa for over thirty-five years. By contrast, my dad died at the age of thirty-four—unhappy and unfulfilled.

I only spent nine years with my father, but they were some of the most influential years of my life. I would learn much later in life that most children perceive God as they perceived their earthly father. I perceived my father as absent—not there when I needed him—not trustworthy.

I often sensed rejection from Dad even while he was alive, and that rejection was reinforced by his death. I saw him as a significant person in my life who abandoned me, though not intentionally.

All parents fall short one way or another. My dad may have fallen short because his parents let him down. Similarly, I too have made mistakes and fallen short of being the godly parent God created me to be. But God never falls short, and that's why He wants us to look to Him to meet certain needs that only He can meet, such as unconditional love and wisdom from heaven.

THE TRUE HEAVENLY FATHER

During my illness, God would reveal His true nature to me—the kind of heavenly Father He really is. Some of that revelation came through the parable of the prodigal son, found in Luke 15:11-24.

> Jesus continued: "There was a man who had two sons. The younger one said to his father, 'Father, give me my share of the estate.' So he divided his property between them.
>
> "Not long after that, the younger son got together all he had, set off for a distant country and there squandered his wealth in wild living. After he had spent everything, there was a severe famine in that whole country, and he began to be in need. So he went and hired himself out to a citizen of that country, who sent him to his fields to feed pigs. He longed to fill his stomach with the pods that the pigs were eating, but no one gave him anything.
>
> "When he came to his senses, he said, 'How many of my father's hired men have food to spare, and here I am starving to death! I will set out and go back to my father and say to him: Father, I have sinned against heaven and against you. I am no longer worthy to be called your son; make me like one of your hired men.' So he got up and went to his father."

Notice that the wayward son came to his senses—realized he had done wrong—and was sorry for it. He wanted to begin doing right, so he chose to go back to his father.

> "But while he was still a long way off, his father saw him and was filled with compassion for him; he ran to

his son, threw his arms around him and kissed him.

"The son said to him, 'Father, I have sinned against heaven and against you. I am no longer worthy to be called your son.'

"But the father said to his servants, 'Quick! Bring the best robe and put it on him. Put a ring on his finger and sandals on his feet. Bring the fattened calf and kill it. Let's have a feast and celebrate. For this son of mine was dead and is alive again; he was lost and is found.' So they began to celebrate."

The truth about God's true nature, as revealed in this story, is that His love is patient. He keeps looking and waiting for us to return to Him. He longs to forgive us, just as the father ran to meet his son. He's filled with joy and compassion when we seek Him, eager to welcome us with His love and acceptance.

The prodigal son's father still loved his son, even though the child was sinning. But the father wouldn't help him until his son wanted help from his father. I learned that the same is true with God. If I was to be helped, I too had to come to my senses, repent of my sin, and return to my Father for His forgiveness and wisdom.

"If you return to the Lord...He will not turn his face from you if you return to him" (2 Chronicles 30:9).

The sooner I understood God's true character, the sooner I could comprehend His love for me and gradually *transfer my trust* to Him.

Lesson #4

God's Love Is Intimate

Three years had passed, and the anxiety and depression continued, which served to reinforce my thinking that God had given up on me. With that mindset, I decided I didn't care any more. *Still trusting myself—still fighting for my freedom*—I decided to spend a night on the town, thinking maybe I could escape the pain for at least a few hours.

I stopped at a couple of nightclubs, but I didn't order any drinks or even sit down. I just walked in, looked around, listened, and thought, "There may be a lot of talking and laughing going on, but there isn't anything here that can take away my pain." So I left.

> "No temptation has overtaken you but such as is common to man; and God is faithful, who will not allow you to be tempted beyond what you are able, but with the temptation will provide the way of escape also, that you may be able to endure it" (1 Corinthians 10:13, NASB).

This was a weeknight, around midnight. Driving alone in a small town late at night, I remember how quiet it was: no other cars, no people, just street lights against the dark sky. I felt all alone.

As I drove along, the hurt and frustration began to build. I knew I didn't want to live an immoral lifestyle, yet walking with the Lord no longer seemed an option. Any flicker of hope God had given me earlier was being extinguished.

But then, on that dark, quiet, lonely night, only a few seconds after those thoughts went through my mind, I came over a hill in the road. As I pulled to a stop at the bottom of the hill, I glanced to my right. There on a giant black billboard stood three words in bright pink letters: "JESUS LOVES YOU."

For years in Sunday school I had sung the words, but they had little meaning.

That night was different. No longer were they just words. That night, they were *His words to me.* I was overwhelmed by the intimate love of God. He had personally given me another flicker of hope that His grace and forgiveness were available to me.

Tears came to my eyes. I thanked Him and went home.

"Praise be to the Lord, for he showed
his wonderful love to me..."
Psalm 31:21

If you're not certain of God's love for you, have never received Jesus Christ as your personal Savior and Lord, or if you're struggling with the assurance of your salvation, please see pages 107-110 of the appendix. There you will find basic truths that the Lord Jesus impressed upon me as I struggled with the assurance of my own salvation.

TRANSFER OF TRUST

Father, without the certainty of Your love and acceptance, it would have been impossible for me to trust You. Thank You for confirming Your love for me in such an intimate way. In Jesus' name, amen.

NEXT

In chapter five, I'm challenged with another choice: to forgive or not to forgive—and to consider the consequences of each decision.

Review

1. As you were growing up, what actions or behaviors by your dad made you feel:

LOVED? _____

SIGNIFICANT? _____

SECURE? _____

2. As you were growing up, what actions or behaviors by your dad made you feel:

UNLOVED? _____

INSIGNIFICANT? _____

INSECURE? _____

3. If you have perceived God to be like your earthly father, how might that pose a barrier that keeps you from *transferring your trust* to God?

_____
_____
_____

4. Have you ever experienced God's love *for you* in an intimate, personal way? Be specific in explaining your answer.

_____
_____
_____

Chapter 5

Will I Choose to Forgive?

"Do not let any unwholesome talk come out of your mouths,
but only what is helpful for building others up according to their
needs, that it may benefit those who listen. And do not grieve
the Holy Spirit of God, with whom you were sealed for the
day of redemption. Get rid of all bitterness, rage and anger,
brawling and slander, along with every form of malice. Be kind
and compassionate to one another, forgiving each other,
just as in Christ God forgave you."

Ephesians 4:29-32

In 1920, my paternal grandparents became pioneer missionaries to Africa. They would visit our family for a few days once every five years while home on furlough in the United States. I have only vague memories of my grandparents and never really got to know them.

What I do remember is that my mom didn't like my grandma. Mom always spoke highly of my grandfather and seemed to have much respect for him. But if you ever mentioned Grandma's name, Mom would bristle up like a cat coming face to face with a dog.

My parents and grandparents are deceased now, so I'll tell you why my mom didn't like my grandmother. I'm not sharing this with you to be critical of either person, but rather to convey an example of the harm that results from a critical spirit and an unforgiving spirit.

Mom described Grandma as a "holier than thou Baptist." I was told Grandma was extremely critical of my mom because she wore lipstick and occasionally wore slacks instead of a dress. Upon learning that my mom and dad went to the movies, Grandma berated them with more harsh, judgmental words.

What hurt Mom the most came after an unexpected surgery. Back in the mid 1940s, shortly after Mom and Dad were married, it was discovered that Mom had a tumor in her back. Mom was blessed to get into Mayo Clinic in Rochester, Minnesota, where the doctor informed her that she desperately needed surgery but that her odds of surviving the operation were not good.

God was kind to my mom. He spared her life, brought her through the surgery and eventually to a full recovery. For a short time following the surgery, however, Mom had a difficult time walking.

How would you expect a godly missionary woman to respond to her daughter-in-law during such a traumatic experience? My grandma responded by trying to get my parents' marriage annulled.

Mom never forgave her mother-in-law. It was bad enough that Mom perceived Grandma to be a hypocritical Christian and was unwilling to forgive her. But what made matters worse was the fact that my mother's bitterness would later be inappropriately directed toward other Christians.

This led to Mom taking us out of the Bible-teaching church that Dad had faithfully taken us to each Sunday.

Like all of us, Mom had a choice to respond to rejection with unforgiveness or to seek to respond supernaturally as Christ did when He looked from the cross at the people who crucified Him and said with compassion, "Father, forgive them, for they do not know what they are doing" (Luke 23:34a).

> "See to it that no one comes short of the grace of God; that no root of bitterness springing up causes trouble, and by it many be defiled" (Hebrews 12:15, NASB).

VIEWING OTHERS FROM GOD'S PERSPECTIVE

In the early stages of my illness, I explored memories from my childhood in an attempt to figure out what was happening. I came to realize that the relationship between my mom and grandma had negatively impacted my life. God began to search my heart, exposing similar sin in my own life.

I've struggled with being too critical of myself and others, but through God's Word and conviction from His Holy Spirit, I'm reminded that none of us have arrived, nor will we ever be filled to the full measure of Christ until we meet Him face to face.

When I was young, I often replayed in my mind ways I'd been hurt by others. But it seldom, if ever, crossed my mind that people who wounded me had likely been hurt when they were growing up. As God revealed this to me, I chose to begin seeing others as I saw myself—people who long to be loved and accepted.

With God's help, I began to see others through the eyes of Jesus Christ—as rejected, hurting people who, like myself, are sinners with weaknesses. Maybe they too had never come to know God as their Father because they had been so rejected by their earthly fathers and didn't know God as the trustworthy and compassionate Father that He is. Perhaps they hadn't come to a knowledge of the truth, especially the truth of God's love for them and how He longs to forgive and reconcile broken relationships.

During my illness, God helped me see the anger I had toward my mom and dad; anger toward Dad because I lived in fear of his temper the first nine years of my life; anger because of being neglected by him and for leaving me father-less and without discipline. My anger toward Mom came from her preferring time partying with her friends to time with me while my dad was living, her failure to discipline me after Dad died, and because she removed my brother and me from our primary source of Biblical truth—the church we attended prior to my dad dying.

Over time, I forgave Mom and Dad. First, because the Bible commands us to *forgive each other just as in Christ God has forgiven us* (Ephesians 4:32). Next, because I had experi-enced the grace and forgiveness of God so intimately and am still reminded by the following passage of Scripture of what it means to forgive as we've been forgiven.

> "At one time we too were foolish, disobedient, deceived and enslaved by all kinds of passions and pleasures. We lived in malice and envy, being hated and hating one another. But when the kindness and love of God our Savior appeared, he saved us, not because of righteous things we had done, but because of his mercy. He saved us through the washing of rebirth and renewal by the Holy Spirit, whom he poured out on us generously through Jesus Christ our Savior, so that, having been justified by his grace, we might become heirs having the hope of eternal life" (Titus 3:3-7).

I learned that God not only wants us to forgive people who have hurt us; He also wants us to respond to them as

He does, with loving compassion, because *"mercy triumphs over judgment"* (James 2:13b).

After hearing stories about Mom and Dad's childhoods, I began to have more love and compassion for my parents.

Dad was a respected man in the town in Michigan where I grew up. He was Justice of the Peace, president of Jaycees, worked two jobs, and was very diligent. He attended church regularly, read the Bible, and believed in Jesus Christ.

My Uncle Bruce informed me that my dad told him that he had been called to be an evangelist. I believe my dad failed to respond to that call from God because he received more love and acceptance from people who were not Christians than people who were. As mentioned earlier, Dad was only eight years old when he was separated from his parents and siblings and left to live with strangers who treated him unkindly. After having been hurt by the separation from his family and mistreated by his "Christian" caregivers, it is my opinion that my dad was unwilling to *transfer his trust* from himself to God, which would have made it possible for him to answer God's call on his life.

I now have some understanding of how painful Dad's early childhood years must have been for him. I've forgiven my dad—I still love him—and I miss him. Most of all, I'm truly sorry that my dad missed God's best for his life.

Mom's story is uniquely different. I learned of a number of ways in which she experienced rejection. She was adopted as a newborn baby, the only child of my grandparents. She admitted to me that she had been a spoiled only child who was rarely disciplined. Mom told me she always wanted to meet her biological parents but didn't because she never wanted to hurt her mom and dad who adopted her. She shared with me that throughout her childhood, her dad never once held her on his lap and never once told her he loved her.

Mom's mother-in-law was harsh and judgmental of her and tried to get Mom and Dad's marriage annulled. Her husband—my dad—died young, and Mom became a widow at the age of thirty-two with two sons, ages nine and eleven, to raise without the help of a husband.

As with Dad, I have compassion for my mom having to endure the various rejections she encountered in life.

I praise God that Mom and I forgave each other and reconciled before she died. I wrote a letter to her before she passed away, thanking her for all the positive things I learned from her. Here are excerpts from that letter:

Dear Mom,

Happy Mother's Day! I thought I would give you a more unique gift this year—a letter from your son.

I just want to share a few memories of my mom and some of the things you taught me, for which I am grateful.

One of the first things that come to mind is that you didn't complain. I think how hard it must have been forty-four years ago when you had to tell two little boys that your husband and our dad had died, knowing we had become your sole responsibility. You didn't complain or share how much you were hurting. You just tried to comfort Fred and I.

You were diligent. I remember how hard you worked as social editor of the newspaper—all the early mornings and late nights in order to get the paper out the next day.

I think of how rough it must have been for you to work so hard and make so many everyday decisions without the support, companionship, love, and help of Dad. And, how difficult it must have been not having him around to discipline a wild son such as I was. But you didn't complain.

As tired as you must have been, you still made time to go to my basketball and football games and were always very supportive in many different ways.

You taught me kindness. You were always very kind to me, my friends, and your friends. I remember you always driving Larry and I out to the lake so we could swim or to the golf course so we could golf, and how you would always have a nice meal for us when we returned. And how you always took your casserole dinners over to your friends who were ill or had a death in the family, just to let them know you cared.

You had and still have the gift of hospitality—hosting all my friends throughout our school years—just letting us hang out together, talking, laughing, and all the good times watching the Olympics—and your great cookin'.

You often encouraged me to live a day at a time—though it took me a long time to understand what that meant, you helped me learn a very important principle.

Something else I've often thought about is when you shared that you would have liked to have met your biological parents. And on another occasion when you told me you couldn't remember one time when Grandpa Rube ever held you on his lap and told you he loved you.

Mom, even though we know Grandma Reina and Grandpa Rube were your parents and loved you the best they knew how, I'm sorry you didn't get to meet your other mom and dad, and I'm sorry that Grandpa Rube didn't know how to express his feelings better. I realize these things seem pretty insignificant now, but they probably weren't as you were growing up.

I remember Fred and I raking leaves with you and jumping in them when we were little, the security of knowing you were home as we played football in our back yard, flew a kite in the parking lot, or sneaked into the old lumber yard. We knew you were there, if we needed you.

You're very generous—not necessarily a good money manager, but you are very generous. You've modeled contentment. When you finally had some money, you gave more to others than you spent on yourself.

Mom, for all you've been through in life, you've done extremely well. You've set an example of kindness, unselfishness, compassion, diligence and hard work, other-mindedness, contentment, and have had just a wonderful love for life and joy in the simple things of life, such as friends, flowers, sunrises, and sunsets.

You know there's much more I could write about, but I mainly want you to know what a tremendous blessing you've been to me over the years, and how grateful I am for your love.

It's been nice thinking of special times with a SPECIAL MOM.

Thank you for all your love and kindness to me.

I Love You, MOM!

The following year, my mom died.

UNDERSTANDING THE CONSEQUENCES OF UNFORGIVENESS

"Then Peter came and said to Him, 'Lord, how often shall my brother sin against me and I forgive him? Up to seven times?'

Jesus said to him, "I do not say to you, up to seven times, but up to seventy times seven.

"For this reason the kingdom of heaven may be compared to a certain king who wished to settle accounts with his slaves.

"And when he had begun to settle them, there was brought to him one who owed him ten thousand talents.

"But since he did not have the means to repay, his lord commanded him to be sold, along with his wife and children and all that he had, and repayment to be made.

"The slave therefore falling down, prostrated himself before him, saying, 'Have patience with me, and I will repay you everything.'

"And the lord of that slave felt compassion and released him and forgave him the debt.'"

We do not have the means to repay God for our sins, yet He has compassion and is willing to forgive us.

"'But that slave went out and found one of his fellow slaves who owed him a hundred denarii; and he seized him and began to choke him, saying; 'Pay back what you owe.'

"So his fellow slave fell down and began to entreat him, saying, 'Have patience with me and I will repay you.'

"He was unwilling however, but went and threw him in prison until he should pay back what was owed.

"So when his fellow slaves saw what had happened, they were deeply grieved and came and reported to their lord all that had happened.

"Then summoning him, his lord said to him,

'You wicked slave, I forgave you all that debt because you entreated me.

'Should you not also have had mercy on your fellow slave, even as I had mercy on you?'

"And his lord, moved with anger, handed him over to the torturers until he should repay all that was owed him.

"So shall my heavenly Father also do to you, if each of you does not forgive his brother from your heart'" (Matthew 18:21-35, NASB).

What is Jesus saying with His words, *"Handed over to the torturers...if each of you does not forgive his brother from your heart"*?

The best explanation I've found is in the following quote from *Improving Your Serve*, by Chuck Swindoll:

> "He [Jesus] is saying the one who refuses to forgive, the Christian who harbors grudges, bitter feelings toward another, will be turned over to torturous thoughts, feelings of misery, and agonizing unrest within. One fine expositor describes it like this:
>
> 'This is a marvelously expressive phrase to describe what happens to us when we do not forgive another. It is an accurate description of gnawing resentment and bitterness, the awful gall of hate or envy. It is a terrible feeling. We cannot get away from it. We feel strongly this separation from another and every time we think of them we feel within the acid of resentment and hate eating away at our peace and calmness. This is the torturing that our Lord says will take place.'"

When I have bitterness toward someone, I grieve the Holy Spirit of God. By choosing not to forgive others, I

suffer both the torment caused by an unforgiving spirit as well as the loneliness, anxiety, and depression that are consequences of being out of fellowship with God.

In terms of my own story, **the only thing I lost when I forgave myself and others was my misery.** Choosing to accept God's forgiveness and to forgive myself and others were both essential to opening the door for God to replace my depression and anxiety with the joy and peace of Christ.

> "The Holy Spirit reveals that God loved me not because I was lovable, but because it was His nature to do so. Now, He says to me, show the same love to others—"Love as I have loved you." "I will bring any number of people about you whom you cannot respect, and you must exhibit My love to them as I have exhibited it to you."
>
> —Oswald Chambers,
> *My Utmost for His Highest*, May 11

Lesson #5

God's Love Extends Grace and Forgiveness

I'm not worthy of God's grace, yet He forgives me. The following story has been an inspiration to me of how to respond to people I might perceive to be unworthy of my grace:

A Love That Would Not Give Up

"At the very least, actively loving an enemy will protect you from being spiritually defeated by anger, bitterness, and a thirst for revenge. And, in some cases, your active and determined love for your opponent may be used by God to bring that person to repentance.

This power was vividly demonstrated during World War II by a Catholic priest named Hugh O'Flaherty, who served in the Vatican during the war. As he learned of Nazi atrocities, he became actively involved in efforts to protect the Jews and to hide Allied pilots who had been shot down over Italy. Colonel Kappler, the German SS commander in Rome, eventually learned of O'Flaherty's activities and set out to kill him. Several assassination attempts failed, but Kappler finally succeeded in capturing several of O'Flaherty's associates. Kappler himself ordered the torture and execution of these prisoners, one of whom was O'Flaherty's closest friend.

When the Allied armies invaded Italy and surrounded Rome in 1944, Colonel Kappler was captured. He was sentenced to life imprisonment for his war crimes. In spite of all the wrongs Kappler had committed, O'Flaherty resisted the temptation to delight in his enemy's downfall. Instead, remembering Jesus' teaching and example, O'Flaherty resolved to love his enemy not only with words, but also with actions. Every month, he drove to Gaeta Prison to see the man who had tried so hard to kill him. Year after year he learned about Kappler's needs and did all he could to meet them. Above all else, he demonstrated to Kappler the love, mercy, and forgiveness of God. In March of 1959, after almost 180 visits from the priest, Kappler finally confessed his sins and prayed with the priest to accept Christ as his Savior."

—Ken Sande, *The Peacemaker*, pp. 202-203

Almost 180 visits—once every month—that's fifteen years of demonstrating the love, mercy, and forgiveness of God to a person who had tried to kill him.

> "Bear with each other and forgive whatever
> grievances you may have against one another.
> Forgive as the Lord forgave you."
> Colossians 3:13

TRANSFER OF TRUST

Father, thank You for Your forgiveness of my sins. Help me to never forget the cost of that forgiveness. I'm grateful that You not only forgive, but You also "remember our sins no more" (Hebrews 8:12).

Father, I praise You for enabling me to forgive others as You have forgiven me. My prayer and desire is that I, through the power of Your Holy Spirit, extend mercy and forgiveness to anyone who may ever wrong me, reject me, or hurt me in any way—so they too can experience Your incomprehensible grace and be drawn near to You. In Jesus' name, amen.

NEXT

I stopped fighting—I began to surrender—I could sense the freedom. In chapter six, I'll share how God's love compelled me to surrender and *transfer my trust* to Him. Was I ready to surrender? The answer would come from my response to this question, *"Do you want to be 'right' or do you want to be well?"*

REVIEW

1. Read Hebrews 12:15, Matthew 18:32-35, and the quote from the book, *Improving Your Serve,* by Chuck Swindoll on page 72. List consequences that result from bitterness and choosing not to forgive.

   _____

   _____

2. First read the section under the subtitle, *Viewing Others From God's Perspective.* Then read Matthew 5:43-45a. Is God's perspective on how to respond to enemies different than yours? If yes, in what ways?

   _____

   _____

3. List the names of anyone you have not forgiven, *including God and yourself.*

   _____

   _____

4. First read Acts 3:19, Titus 3:3-7, Psalm 103:10-12, Isaiah 1:18. Then read Ephesians 4:32 and Colossians 3:13. How does each verse speak to you?

   _____

   _____

5. What action will you take to forgive the person or people you have listed above?

   _____

   _____

Chapter 6

Do You Want to Be "Right" or Do You Want to Be Well?

"Some time later, Jesus went up to Jerusalem for a feast of the Jews. Now there is in Jerusalem near the Sheep Gate a pool, which in Aramaic is called Bethesda and which is surrounded by five covered colonnades. Here a great number of disabled people used to lie—the blind, the lame, the paralyzed. One who was there had been an invalid for thirty-eight years. When Jesus saw him lying there and learned that he had been in this condition for a long time, he asked him, "Do you want to get well?"

John 5:1-6

Like the invalid, God helped me come to the realization that I was out of options with no solution, except for one—**Jesus Christ**—exactly where God wanted me to be!

I SURRENDER

As mentioned earlier, I had a problem with trust. As a result, I didn't believe the counsel or advice of people who were trying to help me.

At that point in my life, when I was convinced I had committed the unpardonable sin and believed I had exceeded God's grace, I was frozen with fear and called every pastor I knew. They assured me that I had not committed the unpardonable sin, yet their words did not help. I didn't believe them. (If you recall, what I perceived to be the unpardonable sin was not one particular heinous sin, but rather a trifling with God's grace to the point where His Holy Spirit leaves for good—no longer to bring conviction of sin.)

Finally, as mentioned in the section titled *Background for Chapter 1*, I went to see my Uncle Bruce, who had been a missionary for many years. He gave me Scriptures and books written by theologians to reassure me that if I had committed the unpardonable sin, my heart would be so hard and my conscience so defiled that I wouldn't even care if I had exceeded God's grace. I didn't believe him.

While visiting my uncle, I talked with the dean, a professor, and the pastoral counselor of a very well known Christian university. They all said the same thing my uncle told me—that I had not committed the unpardonable sin because if I had, I wouldn't care. I didn't believe them either.

One day my uncle said to me, "You know what your problem is? You think you're smarter than all of us." He was right. I did think I was smarter than all of them because I knew myself better than they did. But what I hadn't considered was that they knew the true and living God better than I did.

For three years of my illness, I had picked the Bible apart and read numerous books on emotional healing—listened to sermons in search of just one shred of evidence to give me hope that I was wrong—yet nothing I read or heard brought freedom from this obsession.

As I was reading yet another book one night, something unique took place. Most often, after reading a book, I have a fairly good recollection of the content, but to this day I don't recall the title, author, or anything about that book, except one sentence. It was a question. As I began to read, it was as though God sat down right next to me—and I believe He did—to personally ask me this question, **"Do you want to be 'right' or do you want to be well?"**

I answered, *"I want to be well."*

That intimate moment with God was one of the most significant turning points in my life. For at that very instant, I became teachable—another essential step in *transferring my trust* from myself to God.

I stopped fighting—I began to surrender—I could sense the freedom.

Finally, I began to understand that if I chose to be "right" and trust in my own logic and intellect, I wasn't going to get well. As I took that first step of faith—choosing to tell myself I was wrong—the *transfer of trust* from myself to the Lord Jesus Christ was reinforced.

I stopped believing the lie from Satan, *the father of lies* (John 8:44). I had not committed the "unpardonable sin." Eventually, I came to understand that the only sin that is unpardonable, is the sin of failing to believe in and receive Jesus Christ as one's personal Savior and Lord before they die. So for all those years my thinking was wrong, and it was time to *give up my right to be "right."*

I wanted to be well, **and my heavenly Father knew what was keeping me from being well. Having been intimately acquainted with my life since birth, God was keenly aware that I did not trust anyone, including Him. He also knew that unless I came to know His love for me and His faithfulness to me, I would never come to trust Him. And, if I failed to ever trust God, there would be no hope of me becoming teachable, and obedient to**

Him—no hope of becoming emotionally and spiritually mature—and no hope of being well again.

Why, by that one question from God was I able to surrender, and become teachable? Because God had used the preceding three years to personally help me come to know Him for who He is. My heavenly Father had steadily and patiently been revealing Himself to me in ways that would enable me to know without a doubt how tenderly merciful and compassionate and long-suffering He is because of His love for people, including me. God had prepared me to trust Him, well before His Holy Spirit gently whispered into my ear, *"Do you want to be 'right' or do you want to be well?"*

Lesson #6

**God's Love Exhorts Us to Surrender
and Transfer Our Trust to Him**

When I was sick, I was on two strong medications, one for depression and another for anxiety. I never thought the pills I took for depression ever helped because they did nothing to remove my feelings of hopelessness and despair. However, I do think the pills I took for anxiety were helpful, as they calmed me down enough to be able to think more rationally.

At one point I tried to get off all medication but wasn't able to as the anxiety became too intense without it.

Toward the end of the fourth year of my illness, I went to a Christian medical doctor and said, "I would like to get off this medication. I've tried unsuccessfully, but want to try again. How do you recommend I reduce the dosage?"

The doctor replied, **"Dump it all down the toilet."** *

I did, and God instantly and miraculously lifted both the anxiety and depression. It wasn't anything the doctor said. It was God's grace and timing. He had my undivided attention for four years and enabled me to *transfer my trust* from myself to Him. For four years, I fought for freedom from anxiety. When I surrendered, God set me free.

> "In my anguish I cried to the Lord, and he
> answered by setting me free."
> Psalm 118:5

> "O Lord my God, I will give you thanks forever."
> Psalm 30:12b

* I'm not suggesting that anyone stop taking medication that has been prescribed for them, as it would be poor counsel for anyone who currently needs to be on such medication. However, my doctor's words were wise counsel for me. Why? Because God had achieved His purposes for my illness, which included me getting to know God for who He is—becoming teachable—and *transferring my trust* from myself to Him.

TRANSFER OF TRUST

Father, I'm forever grateful for Your patient, long-suffering love. I praise You for being the intimate, relational God that You are—a heavenly Father who pursues His children. Thank You for preparing my heart for all those years prior to personally asking me the question, "Do you want to be 'right' or do you want to be well?"

Thank You for giving me the grace to surrender and become teachable. In Jesus' name, amen.

NEXT

In chapter seven, I share a few responses in answer to another challenging question, *"Will I become the person God is calling me to be?"*

REVIEW

1. Read John 5:1-6. Why do you think Jesus asked the man who had been an invalid for thirty-eight years the question, "Do you want to get well?"

   _____

   _____

   _____

2. Read the section under the sub-title, *I Surrender.* What might God be asking you to surrender?

   _____

   _____

   _____

3. In what ways has God revealed Himself to you, that have helped you to know Him better and trust Him more?

   _____

   _____

   _____

Chapter 7

Will I Become the Person God Is Calling Me to Be?

"Until we all reach unity in the faith and in the knowledge
of the Son of God and become mature, attaining to the
whole measure of the fullness of Christ."

Ephesians 4:13

"…God's will is that we would bear a family resemblance to His Son. In other words, God's plan is for us to become more and more like Jesus—not physically, of course, but in the way we think and act and treat other people. From all eternity, the Bible says, God's plan was for us 'to be conformed to the likeness of his Son' (Romans 8:29). We are part of His family—and because of that, we should bear His likeness!

"Do you want to know what God's will is for you? *It is for you to become more and more like Christ.* This is spiritual maturity, and if you make this your goal, it will change your life."

—Billy Graham,
The Journey, pp. 78-79

From Salvation to Sanctification

The Holy Spirit revealed to me that my spiritual needs included not only knowing Jesus as my personal Savior (salvation), but also my need to know Him as Lord of my life (sanctification). Why sanctification? Because God longs for me to *become a person who responds as Christ would*, regardless of my circumstances, so that I will bear witness unto Him for God's glory. I've learned that sanctification is a lifelong process in which God brings to our attention areas of our lives in which we're not yet *Christ-like*. He then gives us opportunity to change and to practice responding as His Son would to the situation.

During the fourth year of my illness, I tried to work again. I still wasn't well but wanted to do something, as I had always been a hard, diligent worker prior to becoming ill. I took a job at McDonald's, rode a bike three miles to and from work, and attempted to figure out the right combination of condiments for each customer.

Most of the time, I was whining on the inside—grumbling about having a college degree, yet stuck flipping hamburgers at a fast-food restaurant. Grumbling was not a *Christ-like* response to my circumstances. I should have been more thankful for God's healing to that point, the work He had provided, and what He was teaching me.

Ongoing Lessons in Humility

Even though God had given me practice in humility through work at McDonald's and during my four years at "Nebuchadnezzar University," God knew I needed a refresher course—so He gave me yet another lesson in humility. Why? Because He wants to conform me to the *likeness of His Son*, and one of the greatest attributes of Christ is *humility* (Philippians 2:8).

To supplement my income, I took a job delivering newspapers at 2 o'clock in the morning. I'm an early riser, but prefer 5 a.m. to 2 a.m. Yet each morning I managed to pull myself out of bed, fold newspapers, and begin my route. The whining and complaining returned. *"Why at my age and with a college degree am I stuck out here in the dark, wee hours of the morning having to deliver these newspapers?"* And it got worse! As I looked down at the list of homeowners on my route, I saw that one person wanted his paper delivered not in the driveway, but on the doorstep. I didn't like that a bit. It slowed me down, and I was trying to get back to bed. At the time, it didn't occur to me that it might have been an elderly or disabled person.

Fussing all the way to and from the doorstep, I got back into my car and onto more driveway deliveries. Now we're movin' again. But wait, here's another person who wanted their paper on their doorstep. I asked myself, *"Who do these people think they are that they deserve to have their papers placed on their doorsteps?"*

Suddenly, I heard a gentle whisper, *"Whatever you do, do as unto the Lord."* Upon hearing those words, my heart and my attitude changed immediately, as I had not forgotten what God had done for me. After that experience, I looked forward to getting up early and delivering newspapers, especially to the people who wanted their papers on their doorsteps. As I approached each set of steps, I would gently lay the newspaper onto the concrete and say, *"Good morning, Lord Jesus. I love you!"*

Not only did my heavenly Father teach me another lesson in humility; but it was the first of many lessons He would teach me on becoming a *servant—like His Son* (John 13:14-17).

OPPORTUNITY TO TRUST AND OBEY

Part of God's plan for helping me *transfer my trust* to Him in every area of my life involved money. To see if I trusted Him in regard to stewardship of finances, God laid on my heart His desire for me to stay out of debt. God then gave me an opportunity to see if I would trust Him and obey Him. When I missed the opportunity, God taught me an important lesson on being *obedient, as Jesus was* (John 14:31a).

It took several years for me to get back on my feet financially. During those years I drove several inexpensive, old, and ugly looking cars. I remember one Sunday driving around in a church parking lot with my youngest son, Travis, looking for a parking space as people were filing into church.

I sensed people watching us drive around in this big, faded, nasty gray car that was twice as long as most cars and resembled a military tank. I commented to Travis, "This is kind of embarrassing, isn't it?"

Gently, my son replied, "Dad, it's not kinda embarrassing. It's real embarrassing."

Not long after that I found myself saying to God, *"I'm tired of driving these old vehicles. I'm just gonna buy a nicer car and make the payments."* I went ahead and bought a clean, newer model station wagon that appeared to be in really good shape and ran well—*for awhile*. It didn't take long for God to show me just how serious He was about having me place my trust in Him and His wisdom, rather than taking matters into my own hands by getting what I wanted through debt.

Two months after I purchased the vehicle, God allowed the car engine to blow up. It was bad enough that I ended up having to ride the bus for a year, but the real kicker was that I had to pay for a car I couldn't drive. Praise God! I've been debt free ever since. And God has faithfully met my every need as He promised He would.

God helped me to see that part of the sanctification process—*the process of becoming the person God is calling me to be*—involves small but significant steps of obedience to God that take place when no one else is watching—except a heavenly Father who longs to conform us to the likeness of His Son.

A SONG IN THE DARKNESS

When I'm focused on God's will and Christ's interests, I can then see life's challenges as opportunities to mature in Christ and bear witness unto Him.

God gives us the example of two men who were mature in Christ, knew life on earth was temporary, and understood their purpose for living. As a result, Paul and Silas model a unique response to difficult circumstances (Acts 16:22-34).

> "The crowd joined in the attack against Paul and Silas, and the magistrates ordered them to be stripped and beaten. After they had been severely flogged, they were thrown into prison, and the jailer was commanded to guard them carefully. Upon receiving such orders, he put them in the inner cell and fastened their feet in the stocks.
>
> About midnight Paul and Silas were praying and singing hymns to God, and the other prisoners were listening to them."

Though falsely accused, arrested, beaten and imprisoned, Paul and Silas sang *a song in the darkness* of their prison cells because their hearts overflowed with joy and praise to the God they loved and trusted.

"Suddenly there was such a violent earthquake that the foundations of the prison were shaken. At once all the prison doors flew open, and everybody's chains came loose. The jailer woke up, and when he saw the prison doors open, he drew his sword and was about to kill himself because he thought the prisoners had escaped. But Paul shouted, "Don't harm yourself! We are all here!"

The jailer called for lights, rushed in and fell trembling before Paul and Silas. He then brought them out and asked, "Sirs, what must I do to be saved?"

They replied, "Believe in the Lord Jesus, and you will be saved—you and your household." Then they spoke the word of the Lord to him and to all the others in his house. At that hour of the night the jailer took them and washed their wounds; then immediately he and all his family were baptized. The jailer brought them into his house and set a meal before them; he was filled with joy because he had come to believe in God—he and his whole family."

The supernatural response from Paul and Silas to injustice bore fruit—the salvation of lives—for God's glory. What circumstances has God allowed *you* to be in right now? Falsely accused? Death of a loved one? Divorce? Loss of employment? Rebellious child? Abusive or neglectful parents? Physical or emotional illness?

Will you ask God to show you His will and purpose for allowing you to suffer and experience the pain you are feeling? Are you open to how God might want to use the pain to conform you to the likeness of His Son? Will you prayerfully ask God for His grace and power to respond as Jesus would?

> "For it is commendable if a man bears up under the pain of unjust suffering because he is conscious of God. To this you were called, because Christ suffered for you, leaving you an example, that you should follow in his steps" (1 Peter 2:19, 21).

> "Therefore, since Christ suffered in his body, arm yourselves also with the same attitude, because he who has suffered in his body is done with sin. As a result, he does not live the rest of his earthly life for evil human desires, but rather for the will of God" (1 Peter 4:1-2).

Will people who observe your response in the midst of suffering witness a supernatural response—one that reflects the *life of Christ in you*?

Will you, like Paul and Silas, have *a song in the darkness* that bears fruit for God's glory?

Their example is a wonderful lesson and powerful reminder that painful life experiences provide opportunities to deepen my relationship with God, allowing Him to minister to me with His strength and protection—His comfort and love—His peace and joy—His presence.

Lesson #7

God's Love Compels Us to Follow His Son

God miraculously healed me. Jesus set me free. Having experienced the love and forgiveness of God so intimately, I began to comprehend the enormity of His amazing grace. Such love has compelled me to live my life for Jesus Christ.

> "For Christ's love compels us, because we are convinced that one died for all, and therefore all died. And he died for all, that those who live should no longer live for themselves but for him who died for them and was raised again."
>
> 2 Corinthians 5:14-15

I thank my heavenly Father with all my heart for the past twenty-four years of peaceful life that He has given me to be a friend and follower of Jesus Christ, a father to my two wonderful sons, Rob and Travis, and two very special daughter-in-laws, Sandi and Sarah, and to be Grandpa to my precious grandchildren, Brevin and Sydney.

I praise God for the great honor and privilege to serve as one of His messengers. And I pray that God will use this book and my life as a testimony to His grace in ways that enable people who are suffering with anxiety or depression to have hope in Jesus Christ, who can set them free for God's glory.

TRANSFER OF TRUST

Father, thank You for helping me understand that my purpose on earth is to become more and more like Your Son.

Thank You for continually reminding me to make Jesus Christ Lord of every area of my life so I can respond with His peace and joy in the midst of difficult circumstances.

May You give Your children songs in the darkness, by enabling us to respond supernaturally through the power of Your Holy Spirit. Help us to have a new mindset—one that sees the valleys in life for what they truly are: mountaintop opportunities through which we can deepen our relationship with You. For it is in these times that we see more clearly just how much we need You.

Help us remember that how we respond to life's challenges reveals how closely we've followed Your Son—how well we know You—and whether or not we're becoming the people You are calling us to be, people who bear witness unto Christ for Your glory. In Jesus' name, amen.

NEXT

If it be God's will, a sequel will follow this book with more of what it means to *become the people God is calling us to be.*

REVIEW

1. Share one unique example in your life where God allowed circumstances that provided opportunity for you to grow in Christ and respond as Jesus would. Did you seize the opportunity, or miss it? Explain.

   _____

   _____

   _____

2. *Becoming the people God is calling us to be* flows out of an intimate relationship with God. Check your understanding of how that relationship develops by placing the options on the left below in order from a to e.

OBEY GOD	a. _____
LOVE GOD	b. _____
KNOW GOD AND HIS WAYS	c. _____
TRUST GOD	d. _____
EXPERIENCE GOD'S LOVE	e. _____

3. Read 1 Peter 2:19, 21; 4:1-2. Why do you think Paul and Silas were able to sing *a song in the darkness* after being falsely accused, arrested, beaten and imprisoned?

   _____

   _____

   _____

4. In what way(s) can you respond to your circumstances that will provide evidence that the *transfer of trust* from yourself to God is taking place in your life?

_____

_____

_____

Selected Scripture

INTRODUCTION

"Unless the Lord had given me help, I would soon have dwelt in the silence of death. When I said, 'My foot is slipping,' your love, O Lord, supported me. When anxiety was great within me, your consolation brought joy to my soul" (Psalm 94:17-19).

"Praise be to the God and Father of our Lord Jesus Christ, the Father of compassion and the God of all comfort, who comforts us in all our troubles, so that we can comfort those in any trouble with the comfort we ourselves have received from God" (2 Corinthians 1:3-4).

CHAPTER 1

"Those who live according to the sinful nature have their minds set on what that nature desires; but those who live in accordance with the Spirit have their minds set on what the Spirit desires. The mind of sinful man is death, but the mind controlled by the Spirit is life and peace; the sinful mind is hostile to God. It does not submit to God's law, nor can it do so. Those controlled by the sinful nature cannot please God" (Romans 8:5-8).

"But at the end of that period I, Nebuchadnezzar, raised my eyes toward heaven and my reason returned to me, and I blessed the Most High and praised and honored Him who lives forever....

Now I Nebuchadnezzar praise, exalt, and honor the King of heaven, for all His works are true and His ways just, and He is able to humble those who walk in pride" (Daniel 4:34,37, NASB).

"Draw near to God and He will draw near to you" (James 4:8a, NASB).

"My son, do not reject the discipline of the Lord, Or loathe His reproof, For whom the Lord loves He reproves, Even as a father, the son in whom he delights." (Proverbs 3:11-12, NASB).

"FOR THOSE WHOM THE LORD LOVES HE DISCIPLINES..." (Hebrews 12:6, NASB).

CHAPTER 2

"Behold, Thou dost desire truth in the innermost being, and in the hidden part Thou wilt make me know wisdom" (Psalm 51:6, NASB).

"For it is God who works in you to will and to act according to his good purpose" (Philippians 2:13).

"All Scripture is given by inspiration of God, and is profitable for doctrine, for reproof, for correction, for instruction in righteousness" (2 Timothy 3:16, NKJV).

"Search me, O God, and know my heart; test me and know my anxious thoughts. See if there is any offensive way in me, and lead me in the way everlasting" (Psalm 139:23-24).

"But He said to me, 'My grace is sufficient for you, for my power is made perfect in weakness.' Therefore, I will boast all the more gladly about my weaknesses, so that Christ's power may rest on me" (2 Corinthians 12:9).

"Jesus answered, 'I am the way and the truth and the life...'" (John 14:6).

"Then you will know the truth, and the truth will set you free" (John 8:32).

CHAPTER 3

"So then faith comes by hearing, and hearing by the word of God" (Romans 10:17, NKJV).

"Be anxious for nothing, but in everything by prayer and supplication with thanksgiving let your requests be made known to God. And the peace of God, which surpasses all comprehension, shall guard your hearts and your minds in Christ Jesus" (Philippians 4:6-7, NASB).

"When I was a child, I talked like a child, I thought like a child, I reasoned like a child. When I became a man, I put childish ways behind me" (1 Corinthians 13:11).

"We demolish arguments and every pretension that sets itself up against the knowledge of God, and we take captive every thought to make it obedient to Christ" (2 Corinthians 10:5).

"For God has not given us a spirit of fear, but of power and of love and of a sound mind" (2 Timothy 1:7, NKJV).

"Now this is eternal life: that they may know you, the only true God, and Jesus Christ, whom you have sent" (John 17:3).

"You will keep him in perfect peace, whose mind is stayed on You, because he trusts in You" (Isaiah 26:3, NKJV).

CHAPTER 4

"…God demonstrates his own love for us in this: While we were still sinners, Christ died for us" (Romans 5:8).

"Our fathers disciplined us for a little while as they thought best; but God disciplines us for our good, that we may share in his holiness" (Hebrews 12:10).

"If I had cherished sin in my heart, the Lord would not have listened; but God has surely listened and heard my voice in prayer" (Psalm 66:18-19).

"My dear children, I write this to you so that you will not sin. But if anybody does sin, we have one who speaks to the Father in our defense—Jesus Christ, the Righteous One" (1 John 2:1).

"When he came to his senses, he said, 'How many of my father's hired men have food to spare, and here I am starving to death! I will set out and go back to my father and say to him: Father, I have sinned against heaven and against you. I am no longer worthy to be called your son; make me like one of your hired men.' So he got up and went to his father.

"But while he was still a long way off, his father saw him and was filled with compassion for him; he ran to his son, threw his arms around him and kissed him" (Luke 15:17-20).

"If you return to the Lord...He will not turn his face from you if you return to him" (2 Chronicles 30:9).

"Praise be to the Lord, for he showed his wonderful love to me..." (Psalm 31:21).

CHAPTER 5

"Do not let any unwholesome talk come out of your mouths, but only what is helpful for building others up according to their needs, that it may benefit those who listen. And do not grieve the Holy Spirit of God, with whom you were sealed for the day of redemption. Get rid of all bitterness, rage and anger, brawling and slander, along with every form of malice. Be kind and compassionate to one another, forgiving each other, just as in Christ God forgave you" (Ephesians 4:29-32).

"See to it that no one comes short of the grace of God; that no root of bitterness springing up causes trouble, and by it many be defiled" (Hebrews 12:15, NASB).

"At one time we too were foolish, disobedient, deceived and enslaved by all kinds of passions and pleasures. We lived in malice and envy, being hated and hating one another. But when the kindness and love of God our Savior appeared, he saved us, not because of righteous things we had done, but because of his mercy. He saved us through the washing of rebirth and renewal by the Holy Spirit, whom he poured out on us generously through Jesus Christ our Savior, so that, having been justified by his grace, we might become heirs having the hope of eternal life" (Titus 3:3-7).

"Mercy triumphs over judgment!" (James 2:13b).

"Bear with each other and forgive whatever grievances you may have against one another. Forgive as the Lord forgave you" (Colossians 3:13).

CHAPTER 6

"Some time later, Jesus went up to Jerusalem for a feast of the Jews. Now there is in Jerusalem near the Sheep Gate a pool, which in Aramaic is called Bethesda and which is surrounded by five covered colonnades. Here a great number of disabled people used to lie—the blind, the lame, the paralyzed. One who was there had been an invalid for thirty-eight years. When Jesus saw him lying there and learned that he had been in this condition for a long time, he asked him, 'Do you want to get well?'" (John 5:1-6).

[Jesus said,] "I am the vine; you are the branches. If a man remains in me and I in him, he will bear much fruit; apart from me you can do nothing" (John 15:5).

"In my anguish I cried to the LORD, and he answered by setting me free" (Psalm 118:5).

"O LORD my God, I will give you thanks forever" (Psalm 30:12b).

CHAPTER 7

"Until we all reach unity in the faith and in the knowledge of the Son of God and become mature, attaining to the whole measure of the fullness of Christ" (Ephesians 4:13).

"For those God foreknew he also predestined to be conformed to the likeness of his Son, that he might be the firstborn among many brothers" (Romans 8:29).

"And being found in appearance as a man, he humbled himself and became obedient to death—even death on a cross!" (Philippians 2:8).

[Jesus said,] "Now that I, your Lord and Teacher, have washed your feet, you also should wash one another's feet. I have set you an example that you should do as I have done for you. I tell you the truth, no servant is greater than his master, nor is a messenger greater than the one who sent him. Now that you know these things, you will be blessed if you do them" (John 13:14-17).

[Jesus said,] "But the world must learn that I love the Father and that I do exactly what my Father has commanded me" (John 14:31a).

"For it is commendable if a man bears up under the pain of unjust suffering because he is conscious of God. To this you were called, because Christ suffered for you, leaving you an example, that you should follow in his steps" (1 Peter 2:19, 21).

"Therefore, since Christ suffered in his body, arm yourselves also with the same attitude, because he who has suffered in his body is done with sin. As a result, he does not live the rest of his earthly life for evil human desires, but rather for the will of God" (1 Peter 4:1-2).

"For Christ's love compels us, because we are convinced that one died for all, and therefore all died. And he died for all, that those who live should no longer live for themselves but for him who died for them and was raised again" (2 Corinthians 5:14-15).

Sources and Permissions

The following are the sources of excerpts used in this book:

Chambers, Oswald, *My Utmost for His Highest* (Uhrichsville, OH: Barbour Publishing, Inc.), May 11 entry.

Graham, Billy, *The Journey* (Nashville, TN: W publishing Group, a division of Thomas Nelson, Inc., 2006), pp. 78-79.

Sande, Ken, *The Peacemaker* (Grand Rapids, MI: Baker Book House, 1991), pp. 202-203.

Swindoll, Charles R., *Improving Your Serve* (Waco, TX: Word, Incorporated, 1981), pp. 66-67.

Appendix

Becoming a Forgiven Child of God

1. Repent of Your Sins.

"For the wages of sin is death, but the gift of God is eternal life in Christ Jesus our Lord" (Romans 6:23).

"The Lord is not slow in keeping his promise, as some understand slowness. He is patient with you, not wanting anyone to perish, but everyone to come to repentance" (2 Peter 3:9).

The word *repent* means to change—to change your mind, your attitude, and your way of living. You can't do that alone, but God can help you to change.

"Repent, therefore, and be converted, that your sins may be blotted out..." (Acts 3:19, KJV).

2. Believe in the Lord Jesus.

"...Sirs, what must I do to be saved?"
They replied, "Believe in the Lord Jesus, and you will be saved—you and your household" (Acts 16:30-31).

The word *believe* means much more than intellectual knowledge. It means you believe Jesus is the Son of God (Matthew 26:63-64a), who died for your sins, was buried, and rose from the dead—the Lord who you're willing to trust and obey.

> "For what I received I passed on to you as of first importance: that Christ died for our sins according to the Scriptures, that He was buried, that He was raised on the third day according to the Scriptures" (1 Corinthians 15:3-4).

3. Receive Jesus Christ As Your Personal Savior and Lord.

> "Yet to all who received him, to those who believed in his name, he gave the right to become children of God" (John 1:12).

> "...Everyone who calls on the name of the Lord will be saved" (Romans 10:13).

> "For it is by grace you have been saved, through faith—and this not from yourselves, it is the gift of God—not by works, so that no one can boast" (Ephesians 2:8-9).

4. Confess Christ Openly.

> "That if you confess with your mouth, 'Jesus is Lord,' and believe in your heart that God raised him from the dead, you will be saved" (Romans 10:9).

If you have prayed and *repented* of your sin, *believe* in the Lord Jesus Christ, *received* Him into your heart as your personal Savior, and *confess* Him as your Lord, you're a forgiven child of God—loved and accepted by Him.

> "...God has given us eternal life, and this life is in his Son. He who has the Son has life; he who does not have the Son of God does not have life. I write these things to you who believe in the name of the Son of God so that you may know that you have eternal life."
>
> 1 John 5:11-13

As a forgiven child of God, the following promises are for you:

> "He does not treat us as our sins deserve or repay us according to our iniquities. For as high as the heavens are above the earth, so great is his love for those who fear him; as far as the east is from the west, so far has he removed our transgressions from us" (Psalm 103:10-12).

> "Come now, let us reason together," says the Lord. "Though your sins are like scarlet, they shall be as white as snow; though they are red as crimson, they shall be like wool" (Isaiah 1:18).

It may be difficult for us to believe that God forgives us, accepts us, and loves us because of the way we have been rejected and hurt in the past and also because of guilt over past sins. Some of our old thinking may reoccur, and Satan will try to make us doubt God's love and forgiveness.

Satan, *never* God, will try to make us feel guilt over past sins, try to deceive us into thinking we must suffer longer to pay for our sins, and make us feel unworthy of God's forgiveness. But everyone is unworthy. That's why it's called *grace*.

The truth is always what God says, not what our mind or emotions may try to tell us, or what Satan would try to make us believe—and the truth is: *whoever believes in the Lord Jesus Christ will be saved* (Acts 16:31).

About the Author

Jeff Rosenau is founder and president of Accountability Ministries, which began in 1990, a Colorado-based organization with a national and international reach. Jeff presents seminars and speaks at national conferences, teaching biblical principals that challenge and help prepare God's people to *become the people God is calling us to be,* people who bear witness unto Jesus Christ for God's glory. He has made presentations to leadership and laity at numerous churches and to leadership at a number of parachurch organizations, including Advocates International, Christian Legal Society, Colorado Christian University, Crisis Pregnancy Centers, Denver Seminary, International Student Connection, Peacemaker Ministries, The Christian and Missionary Alliance, The Navigators, and World Venture. He has also shared the ministry's training with pastors and seminary students in Brazil and law students at Handong International Law School in South Korea.

He is author of *Building Bridges Not Walls: Learning to Dialogue in the Spirit of Christ,* published by NavPress, and of the booklet *Christlike Dialogue: Communication That Glorifies God,* published by Peacemaker Ministries.

Jeff resides in Colorado and has two sons, Rob and Travis, two daughters-in-law, Sandi and Sarah, and two grandchildren, Brevin and Sydney.

To learn more about Accountability Ministries, log on to www.accountabilityministries.org.

If you would like to invite Jeff to teach at your congregation or organization, you can contact him in one of the following ways:

Write: Accountability Ministries
14046 East Stanford Circle, I-6
Aurora, Colorado 80015

Call: 303-690-9671

E-Mail: jlr@accountabilityministries.org